THE GU

A History from Beginning to End

Copyright © 2021 by Hourly History.

All rights reserved.

Table of Contents

Introduction

The Middle East in the Twentieth Century

Lead-up to War

The Iraqi Invasion of Kuwait

The World Responds

The Gulf War Begins: Operation Desert Shield

Operation Desert Storm

The Gulf War Ends

Aftermath: The Impact of the Gulf War

Operation Iraqi Freedom

Conclusion

Bibliography

Introduction

The Gulf War occurred between August 1990 and February 1991, when a worldwide coalition of forces responded to an Iraqi invasion of nearby Kuwait. Kuwait is a very small country, but it is incredibly rich in oil, making it one of the most valuable territories in the world. The United States led the response to the invasion, and they are the country most closely associated as the combatant against Iraq in the Gulf War. However, many other nations sent soldiers into battle as well.

The causes of the Iraqi invasion of Kuwait are complex and stretch deep into the history of the Middle East. In large part, the long consequences of centuries of global imperialism are important to understanding this conflict. In addition, competition for control of the world's supply of oil was a major factor in the Iraqi invasion of Kuwait and the Gulf War that followed. Finally, woven into all of this was the issue of religion, not just differences between Muslims and those of other faiths, but also infighting between different groups of Muslims.

The Gulf War was also important because it was the first major global crisis since the beginning of the end of the Soviet Union in 1989. The world looked to the United States, now the undisputed superpower and leader of the "free world," for how to handle crises in this strange new era, where the economic and political threat of communism was at its lowest in more than a century. The Gulf War was the first test.

Once the actual invasion and expulsion operations were underway, the coalition forces were successful relatively quickly. While the casualties they suffered should never be downplayed, the numbers of dead and wounded were relatively low compared to other twentieth-century wars especially. Iraqi deaths among combatants and civilians were higher. In addition, the war caused long-lasting damage to people, infrastructure, and the environment alike.

One of the most controversial and still-debated outcomes of the war was the decision not to orchestrate a coup of Saddam Hussein's government and remove him from power. Coalition forces penetrated deep into Iraq but failed to fully continue into Baghdad (the capital) and remove Hussein from power. This decision was made in large part by U.S. President George

H. W. Bush. That said, the peace agreement that ended the war limited arms and military growth in Iraq for years to come, but there is evidence that these orders were in large part ignored by Hussein's government.

The Gulf War is often remembered because of its connection to the 2003 invasion of Iraq by the United States. In an eerie about-face, the U.S. did in 2003 what they condemned Iraq for in 1990: invading a sovereign foreign nation. After the terrorist attacks on September 11, 2001, U.S. President George W. Bush—the son of George H. W. Bush—vowed to pursue governments that supported terrorism. Based on shaky evidence, the U.S. did what the coalition failed to do in 1991: remove Saddam Hussein from power and institute an ostensibly democratic government. However, they also became mired in a years-long fight.

Chapter One

The Middle East in the Twentieth Century

"The patchwork political landscape of the Arab world—the client monarchies, degenerated nationalist dictatorships, and the imperial petrol stations known as the Gulf states—was the outcome of an intensive experience of Anglo-French colonialism."

—Tariq Ali, Pakistani historian and public intellectual

In order to understand what caused the Gulf War, it is important to go back further and consider the longer history of the Middle East in the twentieth century. In 1900, colonialism was thriving. As they had for hundreds of years, global superpowers (particularly Europeans and the United States) vied to control more territory and natural resources around the world. The oil-rich vastness of the Middle East was growing more valuable, as humans better learned how to exploit fossil fuels and were thus pulled into the worldwide tug-of-war for control of petroleum.

By the outbreak of World War I in 1914, the Ottoman Empire was the major colonial force in the Middle East. With its seat in Constantinople (present-day Istanbul, Turkey), its close proximity to the region helped them maintain control. The Ottomans allied with the Germans in the war, which threw their empire into the conflict between the Germans and the Allies (primarily Britain and France, and later the United States).

Kuwait was of particular interest early in the war. In 1914, it was declared a British protectorate, an act which came after decades of internal political turmoil. Throughout the remaining years of the war, Britain and other Allied countries made vague or dubious promises to various Arab peoples throughout the region that were ultimately largely ignored. At the end of the war, the Allies essentially carved up a great deal of the Middle East and either formally or informally colonized the entire region.

In so doing, they planted the seeds of conflict that would haunt the Middle East later in the twentieth century and into the twenty-first. With their own interests in mind more than anything else, western powers divided the Middle East without taking the people who lived there or natural borders into consideration. This meant that traditionally homogenous ethnic groups were forced apart and thrown in with rivals, which created untold suffering and infighting.

Iraq was a particular site of conflict in the early decades of the twentieth century. Nominally under British control although technically independent, the country struggled to unite its diverse ethnic and cultural groups and establish autonomy. They were finally awarded independence in 1932, but the independence agreement with the British forced them to concede much control, particularly economic.

At the same time, religious tensions in the region were growing. For one thing, just like Christianity, there are many denominations of Islam, and they differ greatly in their interpretations of religious doctrine and what they believe a holy life should look like. This was a chief cause of conflict among ethnic groups throughout the Middle East, and in Iraq in particular. In addition, more and more members of the Jewish faith were migrating to the Middle East, particularly to Palestine, as anti-Semitism and Naziism were on the rise in Europe.

This was no small migration, either. The percentage of Jews in Palestine rose from under 10% to 30% of the total population in a relatively short period of time. This sparked an Arab uprising in Palestine against both the Jews and the British. The British attempted to squash it, but it only ended in 1939 when World War II broke out. Desperate to secure Arab support and avoid internal revolution at the same time, Britain promised the Arabs that they would not support the establishment of a Jewish state in the region and helped curb migration (which wound up being a death sentence for many Jews who were trapped in Europe).

By the end of World War II, Africa (particularly North Africa) and the Middle East were in shambles in more ways than one. Fighting related to the war destroyed infrastructure, killed soldiers and civilians, and ravaged farmland. What was more, the war displaced millions of people; with the religious tensions between various groups of Muslims and Jews especially, the massive movement of peoples only made things worse.

In the first three years after the war, the League of Arab States was established to oppose the formation of a Jewish state in the region, as well as advocate for independence from foreign control (mostly British). At the same time, while the Nuremberg Trials were revealing the magnitude of the atrocities committed against the Jewish people, Zionist cries reached a fever pitch (Zionism is the name of the movement for an independent Jewish state). Jews in Palestine declared war against Britain, and eventually, the newly formed United Nations relented to their demands, forming two separate states: Israel and Palestine. Once again, the west had intervened to draw borders in the region, ignoring many ethnic divides. War and terrorism would plague the region for decades to come.

At the same time as the Middle East was further divided, two more major global phenomena occurred in the wake of World War II. The first was the beginning of the Cold War between the United States and the Soviet Union (and their allies). During this conflict, the superpowers avoided war with each other (which may have meant the use of nuclear weapons) by vying for economic and political influence around the world and by fighting proxy wars in a number of theaters. The Cold War divided the world and ignored nuance. Neither the Americans nor the Soviets accepted the idea that a country could occupy political or economic space outside of capitalism (America) or communism (Soviets); there was no middle ground or alternative.

In addition, a global movement toward decolonization occurred after the end of the war. The reasons for this are both vast and fascinating and too complex for the scope of this narrative. Around the world, regions and peoples fought for autonomy from the west especially, and independence movements tied to the worldwide rise of nationalism sprang up. Through both violent and non-violent means, the global empires of the west broke apart, and the world saw the end of imperialism as they had known it.

As this age of nation-building took place, the United States and the Soviet Union desperately scrambled to control the economic and political systems in these new countries. Both sought allies around the world and adopted an attitude that these new countries were either with them or against them. Both the Soviets and the Americans orchestrated coups, interfered in wars and revolutions, and used covert operations that complicated or disrupted affairs in other sovereign nations. President Bush himself had spent much of his career as director of the Central Intelligence Agency (CIA) and then served as

Ronald Reagan's vice president. Reagan was known as a fierce Cold War hard-liner and involved the U.S. in many covert actions around the world. While these practices sometimes remained hidden during the Cold War in the U.S. and Soviet Union, it was no secret in the places where they took place. Thus, by the time the Cold War ended in the late 1980s-early 1990s, both countries had earned a reputation for interference virtually everywhere in the world.

During the Cold War, Iraq had more closely aligned with the Soviet Union, which made the U.S. suspicious of them, even after the Cold War ended. What was more, Iraq, a primarily Muslim country, opposed Israel and supported the Palestinians in that conflict. Israel was an immensely important ally of the United States in a region where America and Americans were perennially unpopular, but upon which its economy depended for oil. Despite all of this bad blood, though, Iraq became the lesser of two evils in 1980, and the U.S. began working with them.

In the next chapter, we will examine the events in the 1980s that brought the U.S. and Iraq into a tenuous alliance, as well as the forces that broke them apart and resulted in the Gulf War.

Chapter Two

Lead-up to War

"The ruling family in Kuwait is good at blackmail, exploitation, and destruction of their opponents. They had perpetuated a grave U.S. conspiracy against us . . . stabbing Iraq in the back with a poisoned dagger."

—Saddam Hussein

In 1979, the United States placed Iraq on a list of state sponsors of terrorism, right around the time that a man named Saddam Hussein Abd al-Majid al-Tikriti came to power. Hussein would be at the center of Iraqi politics and foreign relations with the United States for more than 30 years.

Also around this time, the Iranian Revolution broke out in Iran. In this revolution, a coalition of Islamic republicans, students, leftists, and other pro-Islamic groups came together to overthrow the Shah of Iran and institute a new government. The U.S. had supported the Shah and had been instrumental in overthrowing his predecessor,

Mohammad Mosaddegh, in 1953, putting the Shah on the throne in the first place.

Barely a year after the culmination of the Iranian Revolution and the institution of Ayatollah Khomeini as the country's leader, Iraq invaded Iran. Ostensibly, they did so to prevent the revolution from spilling over into their own country, but in reality, Hussein hoped to take advantage of the internal and foreign relations chaos created during the revolution. For one thing, Hussein believed that a military victory would come swiftly since the country was barely on its feet after the revolution. But for another thing, Iran had lost the support of the United States and Israel, and Hussein saw this as an opportunity to become the dominant power in the Middle East. What proceeded in the Iraq-Iran War was extremely complex, and fighting continued for eight years. This narrative will focus only on the aspects of this conflict that directly impacted the invasion of Kuwait and the involvement of the United States.

As was their habit during the Cold War, the United States remained officially neutral in this war while covertly supporting one side over the other. In an about-face, they provided supplies, funds, and even some weapons to the Iraqis.

Since the Iranian Revolution had been blatantly anti-American (several Americans were even taken hostage in the embassy when the Shah's government fell), the situation made strange bedfellows of the U.S. and Iraq. The U.S. removed Iraq from their list of state-sponsored terrorism so that they could open full diplomatic relations with them, even though the condemned practices that had earned Iraq a spot on that list had not changed.

The United States was not the only country that Iraq relied on during the Iraq-Iran War. They borrowed a great deal of money from both Kuwait and Saudi Arabia and were deeply in debt by the time of the ceasefire agreement in 1988. This was one of several factors and events between the Iraq-Iran War and the invasion of Kuwait that made invading Kuwait so appealing to Hussein in the first place. Not only would he void Iraq's debts to Kuwait, but he believed he might also be able to negotiate forgiveness or pay off debts to the Saudis as well.

Iraqi relations with other Middle East neighbors became more strained in these intervening years. For one thing, contractors and migrants poured into Iraq during the war, as the conflict created a great number of jobs. Suddenly, though, those jobs disappeared, and at the same time, Iraq demobilized 200,000 troops who all needed employment. Violence and even acts of terror were committed against nationals of other countries within Iraq's borders. Even the government of Iraq became well-known for using torture against prisoners and dissidents.

In addition, issues within OPEC (Organization of Petroleum Producing Countries) further strained Iraq's relations with other members, as well as impeded Iraq's ability to pay off their debts from the war. OPEC placed limits on how much oil could be sold in order to control prices, keeping them high. However, some other countries—notably Kuwait and the United Arab Emirates—over-produced, driving down the price of oil by flooding the market. This hurt Iraq greatly, since they were unable to match the overproduction and thus lost millions of dollars because of the fall in prices per barrel.

Finally, Iraq claimed that Kuwait rightfully belonged under their control because of the way territory was divided during the Ottoman Empire. At that time, the land that would become Iraq and Kuwait was unified under the province of Basra. Iraqis claimed that because of that, there never should have been a division in the first place.

How much this idea was actually believed by those in power in Iraq is unknown; it may have functioned better as a justification for war rather than an actual cause of it. Another point of territorial contention was control of the Rumaila oil field, a massive oil field located only 20 miles from the Kuwait-Iraq border. While technically in Iraq, Hussein alleged that Kuwaitis had been illegally extracting oil in the area, in the very small corner of the fields that lies inside Kuwait.

By the late 1980s, the world was experiencing change at an exponential rate. As we have seen, the Cold War between the United States and the Soviet Union had dictated foreign relations, economics, and more for a generation of people. With the breakup of the Soviet Union and the seeming failure of communism, it was unclear what the world should focus on next. In addition, the fall of the Soviet Union distracted from the events unfolding in the Middle East. Soon, though, the world's attention would again be directed to the region, and the United States would be in a position to lead the response to the first global crisis since the end of the Cold War.

Chapter Three

The Iraqi Invasion of Kuwait

"I saw Kuwait many times before the war. I remember it as a beautiful place, full of very nice people, and it's a tragedy to see that somebody could set out to deliberately destroy a country the way the Iraqis have."

—Norman Schwarzkopf

Kuwait is one of the smallest nations in the Middle East and had it not been for the Iraqi invasion and the Gulf War, many of us may never have even heard of it. But when Iraq invaded this tiny country, they set off a series of events with extremely long-lasting effects.

The invasion of Kuwait in 1990 did not exactly come as a surprise. Even though everyone was distracted by the events in Eastern Europe surrounding the collapse of the Soviet Union, there were still several warning signs that war was a distinct possibility between Iraq and Kuwait. In the previous chapter, we discussed escalating tensions between the two countries and other circumstances (particularly in Iraq) that also contributed to the war. In July of 1990, several more events occurred.

First and most blatant, Iraq moved approximately 30,000 troops to the Persian Gulf, near its border with Kuwait. This was of great concern not only to Kuwait but to the United States and the other Arab countries in the immediate vicinity, including Saudi Arabia, Iran, Syria, United Arab Emirates, and Bahrain. Secondly, Saddam Hussein and his government were growing increasingly paranoid about a conspiracy against them, and in their defense, they were not completely wrong. Syria, located along Iraq's northwest border, had indeed planned an airstrike against Iraq that was prevented at the last minute, avoiding potential catastrophe.

Finally, Iraq's debts continued to plague the country. Debt is an interesting topic in Islam. On the one hand, the Quran advises against amassing debt, but on the other hand, it praises and encourages forgiveness of debts. Hussein lobbied on more than one occasion that Iraq's fellow Muslim nations should uphold this value and forgive the debts, but they refused to do so, especially in an era of ascendent capitalism.

As tensions escalated through the summer, the United States prepared for war by sending troops, supplies, and ammunition (including aircraft carriers) into the Persian Gulf, which quite possibly escalated Hussein's paranoia. Meanwhile, Iraq participated in talks held in Saudi Arabia at the end of July, and it appeared that the conflict would resolve peacefully. However, Iraq demanded that Kuwait pay them $10 billion restitution for the use of the Rumaila oil field. When Kuwait responded by offering only $500 million, Iraq readied itself for war. Just days later, on August 2, 1990, Iraq commenced bombing Kuwait City, the nation's capital.

Iraqi forces began the ground invasion a few hours later. Kuwait shares a border with Iraq along its entire northern and part of its western boundaries, and Iraq entered Kuwait moving in two directions. First, they began at the northern border and moved directly south toward the capital city along one of the country's major highways. Next, they came in from the west, and this second attack was intended to cut off Kuwait City, preventing help from coming from Saudi

Arabia, which shares a border with Kuwait to the south.

The first major engagement of the invasion was the Battle of the Bridges on August 2. It occurred in a town west of Kuwait City along Highway 70. Kuwaiti forces attempted to stop the Iraqis from proceeding, and they were able to delay them and cause some losses (including losses to Iraq's artillery) but were ultimately unable to stop their advance. What the battle revealed, however, was that even though Iraq had a lot of soldiers and arms, they weren't as well organized or battle-ready as they appeared to be.

Generally speaking, though, Iraq encountered little real resistance to their invasion. Within barely a day, they penetrated the capital, including the royal palace. The king's brother was killed, and the rest of the royal family, along with many members of the Kuwaiti military and government officials, fled south to Saudi Arabia. The Kuwaiti military tried to resist the invasion, but at the time, they had less than 20,000 soldiers (compared to Iraq's more than 1 million) and far inferior weaponry and artillery. Hussein next installed his cousin, Ali Hassan al-Majid, as governor of Kuwait. Members of armed forces ransacked Kuwaiti banks, stealing hundreds of millions of dollars. In addition, Hussein took over the Kuwaiti currency (the dinar), making it equal to Iraq's currency, which decimated its value.

The world watched in horror as the events in the Middle East unfolded. Some regarded Hussein as a madman who would stop at nothing to control the majority of the region's wealth, especially its oil fields and reserves. At the same time, since the United States had emerged from the Cold War as the undisputed global superpower, the world looked to America for how to respond.

Chapter Four

The World Responds

"I can tell you this: If I'm ever in a position to call the shots, I'm not going to rush to send somebody else's kids into a war."

—George H. W. Bush

The United States was led through the 1980s by President Ronald Reagan, whose controversial economic and foreign relations policies sparked much debate. Reagan favored taking a hard line against the Soviets and global communism and aggressively interfered in world affairs, including the governmental affairs of other sovereign nations.

It was his vice president, George H. W. Bush, who would lead the world through the actual collapse of the Soviet Union; he succeeded Reagan as president and was inaugurated in January of 1989. Many expected him to follow in Reagan's footsteps, but especially as the end of the Cold War dawned, Bush recognized that he was in a unique position that carried immense responsibility; his actions, he knew, would help shape foreign policy for years to come.

Bush and the United States had actually started planning for a war in the Middle East several years prior. During the Iraq-Iran War, world leaders discussed various options should that conflict spill into other countries, including Kuwait, which they expected that it would. Therefore, the United States and its allies had already considered the possibility of war in the region and begun to make tentative plans for a number of scenarios. A more concrete plan was drawn up (Bush was active in this process during his time as vice president), other powerful nations agreed to it (including Great Britain, led by Margaret Thatcher, who transitioned out of power in 1990), and it became the starting point for the global response to the invasion of Kuwait in 1990.

It quickly became clear that the world would not sit idly by and allow Saddam Hussein to take control of the government of Kuwait or its oil fields. The United Nations held a meeting of its Security Council the day of the invasion, hours after it began. They quickly passed Resolution 660, which condemned the actions of Iraq and demanded that they withdraw from Kuwait and allow the previous government to be reinstituted. Over the course of the conflict, the UN Security Council would pass 11 more resolutions that supported the coalition response. In addition, the Arab League, an organization of nations in the Middle East, also condemned the invasion and demanded Iraq withdraw immediately and unconditionally. The UN then proceeded with diplomatic means in an attempt to end the conflict without further bloodshed.

Obviously, it was unsuccessful. Hussein ignored the resolution, so a few days later, on August 6, the UN passed Resolutions 661 and 665, which enforced economic sanctions against Iraq by authorizing a naval blockade in the Persian Gulf. Hussein finally responded to the calls to action against him six days later, when he issued a statement in which he agreed to withdraw from Kuwait, under conditions he knew would not be met, including the withdrawal of all foreign forces from anywhere in the Arab world. Specifically, he called for Israeli troops to be withdrawn from Lebanon, Palestine, and Syria. This was outrageous, given that the conflict between Israelis and Palestinians was very controversial, and Hussein knew that several countries, including the United States, wouldn't touch it.

Soon, though, Hussein made somewhat more reasonable attempts to negotiate a withdrawal from Kuwait, though his demands were still unlikely to be met. What was more, for many reasons, the United States and other nations would not negotiate with Iraq or make concessions to a country committing an act of aggressive war. They did not want to set a precedent that a country could benefit in any way from committing such acts. Many of the leaders in power at the time, including Bush and Thatcher, well-remembered the Second World War and feared conceding to Hussein in a similar way that the world had conceded to Adolf Hitler.

Then, On November 29, the United Nations issued Resolution 678, which set a deadline of January 15, 1991, for complete Iraqi withdrawal from Kuwait. World leaders at the United Nations also feared that Hussein would not stop with Kuwait and that he would seek to control more and more of the Middle East. At this point, what the world had feared began to look more likely: to stop Hussein and Iraq from continuing to occupy Kuwait and extend their reach, military action would be necessary.

Chapter Five

The Gulf War Begins: Operation Desert Shield

"You Americans, you treat the Third World in the way an Iraqi peasant treats his new bride. Three days of honeymoon, and then it's off to the fields."

—Saddam Hussein

Almost immediately after Iraq invaded Kuwait, the United States and the United Nations began establishing a coalition to respond to the Iraqi act of war. Of chief concern to the United States was that they would not bear the entire financial burden of whatever military action was to come, which was almost certain to be very expensive. Therefore, the U.S. sent an envoy on an international tour to drum up support for the coming war. Their first stop was to Saudi Arabia, which was the other country that bordered Kuwait and where the Kuwaiti royal family and government officials had sought asylum.

Saudi Arabia was a good place to begin because both the Americans and the Saudis feared that Hussein intended to invade there next, threatening Saudi oil fields close to Kuwait in particular. These fears were not baseless, either. Hussein had made several statements against the Saudis, among them claiming that the Saudi state was unworthy of the holy cities of Mecca and Medina. What was more, Iraq owed Saudi Arabia billions of dollars from its war against Iran and did not feel that they should have to repay this debt since the Saudis had also benefited from Iraq's actions against the Iranian Shia government.

Operation Desert Shield was the codename given to the defensive military initiatives that the United States undertook to protect Saudi Arabia. The U.S. was deeply dependent on oil from the Middle East, and if Iraq gained control of Arabian oil fields, some of the largest of which were located close to Kuwait, it could cause a dramatic spike in the price per barrel of oil and send the U.S. economy into a tailspin. What was more, unrest and war in the region in general represented a threat to other U.S. interests, so it was of great importance to them to contain it.

A decade earlier, U.S. President Jimmy Carter (who preceded Reagan) issued what came to be known as the Carter Doctrine, which vowed that the U.S. would defend its own interests in the Persian Gulf. It was in fulfillment of the Carter Doctrine that the U.S. acted to protect Saudi Arabia. Within a week, the United States stationed aircraft carriers and battleships in the Persian Gulf, along with scores of troops from the army, navy, air force, and special forces in Saudi Arabia. In total, more than half a million troops were deployed to the region under Operation Desert Shield alone, a massive response. Iraq tried to stop them by causing a massive oil spill in the Persian Gulf waters, but this, too, was unsuccessful.

In total, the United States was joined by troops from 39 countries around the globe, including Australia; Argentina, Canada, and Honduras from North and South America; Niger and Sierra Leone from Africa; the United Kingdom, France, and Norway from Europe; Singapore and South Korea from Asia; and Qatar, Syria, and the United Arab Emirates from the Middle East. Of course, Kuwait and Saudi Arabia also joined the coalition. The Soviet Union was conspicuously absent, but that was also because they were mired in the collapse of communism and the breakup of their eastern bloc.

The United States and the other coalition countries used several arguments to persuade their publics that answering the Iraqi attack on Kuwait was not only justified but also necessary. The biggest and most understandable argument was that Iraq had violated Kuwait's sovereignty. Many remembered with fear the events of the 1930s, as Hitler and his German army invaded and annexed country after country around Europe before others intervened to stop him. Political leaders warned that allowing Hussein to invade his neighbors unimpeded might eventually plunge the world into another costly, devastating war; therefore, it was better to stop him early.

This idea was all the more frightening because of another justification used to defend the counter-offensive: Saddam Hussein and his government were well-known to have used torture and other punishments outlawed by the Geneva Convention. Human rights abuses in Iraq under Hussein's government were fairly well-publicized by this point, and many people around the world—both leaders and average citizens—

agreed that he and his government were dangerous. In addition, Iraq had employed the use of chemical and biological weapons not only against Iran during the Iraq-Iran War but against an ethnic minority within his own country, the Kurdish people. Many suspected that he was in the process of developing nuclear weapons as well; the world lived in fear of nuclear war throughout the Cold War, so this was especially frightening.

As the United Nations' January 15 deadline approached, much of the world was prepared to go to war against Iraq. Hussein made a last attempt to negotiate, but once again, the U.S. and UN were unwilling to concede anything but a complete and unconditional withdrawal from Kuwait and restoration of all conditions from before the invasion. Therefore, the Gulf War was about to formally begin.

Chapter Six

Operation Desert Storm

"The great duel, the mother of all battles has begun . . . The dawn of victory nears as this great showdown begins."

—Saddam Hussein, January 17, 1991

Operation Desert Storm was the United States codename given to the anti-Iraqi counter-offensive in Kuwait and surrounding areas. It is the phase of the Gulf War that involved actual combat. It was led by American General Norman Schwarzkopf, and it began almost immediately after the deadline set forth by the United Nations passed. On January 16, the UN-led coalition began the counter-offensive with the most massive bombing campaign in military history.

The air offensives bombed three main categories of targets, all of them strategic military sites, including aircraft carriers and anti-aircraft missiles, weapons research and manufacturing facilities, and naval outposts and communication centers. In addition, the coalition actively sought Scud missile launchers, which were small missile launchers widely exported by the Soviet Union during the Cold War. They were capable of being transported on trucks, which posed a significant threat to the coalition military, who deployed covert special forces throughout Iraq and Kuwait to locate them so they could be destroyed. They were easy to hide under bridges or tarps and thus very difficult to find.

Before the coalition began its bombing campaign, Saddam Hussein and his government were very clear that if the United Nations proceeded with military action against their invasion of Kuwait, they would extend hostilities to other western allies, specifically Israel and Saudi Arabia. Mere hours after the bombing commenced, they made good on that promise by launching the first of 88 missiles into Israel. By attacking Israel first, Hussein hoped to ignite the sparks of religious conflict. Remember, Israel was a specifically Jewish state; Hussein hoped that if Israel went to war directly against Iraq, it would force other Arab nations out of the coalition because they would be reluctant to take Israel's side.

His hopes were not fulfilled, however. For one thing, the Scud attacks on Israel weren't very accurate. For another, the United States responded immediately to attempt to protect Israel. While the Iraqis destroyed property with the missiles, casualties were relatively few: under 250 injured and less than 100 killed. Israel also armed all of its citizens with gas masks in the event that Iraq used chemical or biological weapons against them, but that also never happened. Saudi Arabia did the same, and Scud attacks into their country were even less destructive than in Israel.

Hussein-led Iraq tried other methods to stop an attack by western or UN troops. As mentioned previously, on January 23, they intentionally dumped 400 million gallons of crude oil into the Persian Gulf in order to stop a marine invasion and make the waters impassable. The oil was American-owned and worth billions of dollars; it is also important to remember how crucial control of oil reserves was to the causes of this conflict in the first place. What is more, the spill caused unimaginable damage and destruction to wildlife and the natural environment in the area. Nonetheless, this attempt was ineffective.

As the air campaign was drawing to a close, Iraq invaded Saudi Arabia along Kuwait's southern border, starting the Battle of Khafji. The decision to invade Saudi Arabia rather than Israel was almost purely logistical; Israel was too far away, and invading Israel would likely have necessitated war with Jordan (located between them) as well.

The battle began on January 29 and lasted only three days; Saudi forces, supported by American marines, drove Iraqis back across the border. The engagement saw artillery and infantry involvement, but it was first and foremost a demonstration of how effective air support could be for this kind of battle. Iraq suffered far more casualties in this battle, in large part because of the effective use of airstrikes against their invading forces. Despite the fact that Iraqi soldiers were forced back into their own country, fighting continued along the Saudi-Iraqi border throughout the war.

Coalition forces were flooding into Saudi Arabia at this time because Saudi Arabia shares long borders with both Kuwait and Iraq. On February 15, the United States Army began its ground combat operation against Iraq by breaching the border, sending Task Force 1-41, which was a combination of American army divisions led by Lieutenant Colonel James Hillman. These forces (most of them American) along the Saudi border with Iraq were under almost constant artillery fire. They also feared Scud missiles and even biological or chemical weapons. Fighting continued over the next two weeks, with several small battles (particularly tank battles) taking place.

One of the more major engagements in this arena of the war was the Battle of Norfolk on February 27. This battle played a large part in the liberation of Kuwait, which is discussed in the next chapter. It occurred at the very end of the war and dealt a huge blow to Iraq. The coalition destroyed almost 1,000 Iraqi tanks, captured more than 2,500 prisoners, and decimated other vehicles and supplies in the area.

The use of large weaponry and artillery was particularly important in the Gulf War. Armored tanks were used a great deal throughout the conflict, with at least three of the largest tank battles in military history taking place. The Battle of Norfolk was one of them, along with the Battle of Medina Ridge and the Battle of 73 Easting.

Other tank battles included the Battle of Kuwait International Airport, the Battle of Rumaila, and the Battle of Phase Line Bullet.

Both the air and ground campaigns were successful for the coalition forces. Again, Iraq appeared more ready for war than they actually were; they were well-supplied but not well organized or trained. The coalition stopped the invasion of Saudi Arabia and greatly weakened Iraq's ability to continue to wage war. The next phase of the war would obviously be the liberation of Kuwait. Just because Iraqi forces were weakened and struggled against the coalition forces, that did not mean that the war was over. Far from it, in fact, as the Iraqi occupation of Kuwait held strong and posed a significant threat to the achievement of the United Nations' goals.

In some ways, the liberation of Kuwait encompasses the entire war—that was the main goal of the Gulf War, after all. But actual entry into and through the country was difficult and dangerous. Iraq had prepared well for this, peppering Kuwaiti terrain with barbed wire fences, land mines, and other impediments. The coalition forces also greatly feared an attack using chemical or biological weapons.

Nonetheless, the liberation campaign began early in the morning on February 24. Once they were in the country, the U.S. and the rest of the coalition forces encountered little resistance from the Iraqis (and were generally welcomed by the Kuwaiti people who remained in Kuwait). Some fighting took place, but for the most part, Iraqi soldiers surrendered. One exception was over control of the very important Kuwait International Airport, where an actual battle occurred during the liberation.

Hussein himself finally ordered the withdrawal of his troops three days later, on February 27. Now the world faced an even more critical question: Would the coalition continue into Iraq? Would they remove Saddam Hussein from power? With Cold War politics no longer dictating global foreign affairs, the answer was still unclear.

Chapter Seven

The Gulf War Ends

"True courage is being afraid, and going ahead and doing your job anyhow; that's what courage is."

—Norman Schwarzkopf

Now that the Iraqi military and government forces were forced to leave Kuwait, world leaders—particularly George H. W. Bush—faced a crucial question: what to do about Saddam Hussein?

Coalition forces had already made inroads into Iraq by the time Hussein ordered his forces in Kuwait to retreat, especially along the Saudi border, where fighting had been ongoing. During the first couple of weeks of February, small units were sent secretly into Iraq to locate and destroy Scud launchers and other tactical sites. Then, on February 15, the Battle of Wadi Al-Batin began in Iraq and lasted for five days. It was meant to be something of a decoy attack since the actual coalition invasion of Iraq was planned to take place elsewhere. By some measures, it worked, but the Iraqis fought fiercely, causing several American casualties. The American forces withdrew in this battle.

Meanwhile, Iraq turned to their old allies, the Soviets, to help negotiate a ceasefire. The UN rejected the Soviet plan, which would have given the Iraqis much more time to position troops back to pre-invasion levels. Instead, the United Nations gave Iraqis only 24 hours on February 22 to withdraw from Kuwait before resuming warfare, though they ostensibly afforded safe passage to retreating soldiers. By the end of the day on February 23, more than 500 Iraqi soldiers were captured after fighting resumed.

The following day, February 24, American forces crossed the Kuwait-Iraq southern border into Iraq and met little resistance. However, the main offensive was planned for the western border. Earlier on the same day, many more troops (many of them American and French) also entered Iraq on that border, surprising the Iraqi forces there. At the same time, more than 2,000 troops parachuted or landed behind the border via helicopter. These soldiers headed off fleeing Iraqi forces, and some fierce fighting occurred. By the end of the day, thousands of fleeing Iraqi soldiers had been captured and a vital supply line to the troops near Kuwait was intercepted. It came at a cost, though: several coalition members were killed in the fighting.

Over the next couple of days, the coalition forces penetrated deeper into Iraq and covered more ground throughout Kuwait itself. Along the way, their goal was to cripple the Iraqis' ability to wage war or return to Kuwait after the war ended. Hussein and the Iraqi government had not yet surrendered, so the coalition and the United Nations were not sure what would happen if they simply vacated the area. Along the way, they met a huge amount of resistance, much more than they had experienced earlier in the war. While fighting in Saudi Arabia and Kuwait, Iraqi forces typically surrendered when their heavy artillery and tanks were destroyed, but that didn't happen as often during this stage of fighting, probably because so much of it was on Iraqi home turf.

February 25 was the deadliest day for American forces. As the coalition worked to remove Iraqis from Kuwait, an Iraqi Scud missile hit American barracks in Saudi Arabia, killing 28 soldiers and other personnel. Still, coalition forces continued to sweep through Kuwait and into Iraq. The following day, Iraqi troops set more than 700

Kuwaiti oil wells on fire, costing millions of dollars in loss and damages, not to mention immense environmental destruction.

The retreat from Kuwait back through their own country was not always peaceful for Iraqi soldiers. The retreat was very long and somewhat disorganized, which meant that it was sometimes hard for coalition forces to know whether the soldiers were peaceful or not. Highway 80, a six-lane highway from Kuwait to Iraq, became known as the Highway of Death because thousands of retreating Iraqis were killed on it while being pursued by primarily American, British, and French forces.

Finally, by the end of the month, this process was complete. American President Bush declared a ceasefire on February 28 and also declared victory in the Gulf War. Yet perhaps the most controversial moment of the war was still to come: the decision not to pursue Saddam Hussein and remove him from power and not to replace his government with one more favorable to the U.S. and the rest of the coalition. This was a sharp turn away from Cold War politics and remained a topic of much debate for decades to come.

In reality, this decision was not Bush's alone. The United Nations and most of the leaders of the coalition members agreed that overthrowing a government was not the right thing to do and set a dangerous precedent for the post-Cold War era. More than that, though, it was a practical decision. It would have cost an enormous amount of money, and even more importantly, many more lives, both Iraqi and coalition soldiers.

With other domestic and foreign relations issues at hand, the choice to leave Iraq was finalized, but not without imposing strict restrictions on Hussein's ability to wage war in the future. Iraq was limited in military build-up in much the same way that Japan and Germany were after World War II. Numbers of active-duty troops and stores of weapons were strictly limited to what the United Nations believed the country needed only to defend itself. However, these sanctions were incredibly unpopular, especially in such a volatile region, and Hussein's government rarely abided by them. That said, Iraq was contained. It has not since actively attacked another country.

Chapter Eight

Aftermath: The Impact of the Gulf War

"I can see that in the future we will meet another time, no matter what happens, what takes place, and I hope that the Iraqi people and American people will live in peace and have a relationship that express their national interests without one side harming the other."

—Saddam Hussein

The Gulf War had an enormous global impact on many areas of life. For one thing, peace did not return to Iraq once the war was over. Members of the coalition, most notably Americans, had used covert operations to insinuate (or sometimes directly state) that the U.S. would support uprisings in Iraq itself.

In the aftermath of the ceasefire, uprisings occurred in southern Iraq (near Saudi Arabia); war in southern Iraq began practically as soon as the Persian Gulf War ended. In northern Iraq, a rebellion also broke out among the Kurds, an ethnic minority. Both uprisings were brutally squashed by Hussein and his government. Nowhere was this more true than in the Kurdish territory; Hussein's government used chemical and biological weapons against the Kurds, as well as torture and other brutal techniques. For these people, the aftermath of the war was horrific.

Violence in the wake of the Persian Gulf War was not limited to Iraq. When Iraq invaded Kuwait, they initiated a forced migration of Palestinians (already displaced from the establishment of Israel and turmoil in other parts of the Middle East) out of Iraq through intimidation, harassment, and violence. When the royal family of Kuwait returned to power, they not only did nothing to stop this process, but they actually formalized it, expelling as many as 200,000 Palestinian Jordanian citizens from Kuwait. This led to further divisions and rivalries in the already explosive Middle East.

While the war ended relatively quickly, the effects on soldiers on both sides did not end when the ceasefire was signed. In addition to some suffering from post-traumatic stress disorder, in the months following the war and the soldiers' return home, a mysterious illness dubbed "Gulf War Syndrome" plagued military personnel. Scores of soldiers were falling ill with a plethora of symptoms, the most common being gastrointestinal distress, fibromyalgia, and extreme, chronic fatigue. Years later, researchers would also observe what appeared to be a trend in birth defects in children of Gulf War veterans. The source of this illness, which has been devastating for those impacted and their families, remains somewhat of a mystery. Some suspect the use of chemical or biological weapons or exposure to materials used to manufacture them.

Some of these effects may also be attributed to the use of depleted uranium by the U.S. military for their tanks during the Persian Gulf War; as we have seen, tank warfare was very important in this conflict. At the time, the long-term effects of using this type of weapon were not known. The hope was that, because it was depleted, the uranium would not have the same degree of radioactive effects. Although it is still not known definitively how much, if any, depleted uranium takes a toll on long-term health, it appears to have caused some complications for not only veterans of the Gulf War but also civilians in Kuwait and Iraq who were exposed to it. It is another example of the ways in which warfare can have very long-lasting and devastating impacts long after peace agreements are signed.

Another event that caused much controversy was the bombing of civilian infrastructure in Iraq. On the one hand, civilian infrastructure can become collateral damage in any war, and in a war that ended as quickly as the Gulf War, it is natural to wonder what the costs would have been had the war gone on longer. On the other hand, though, there is evidence that some targets were hit not for their strategic importance but to cripple the Iraqi economy and destroy morale to fight. This disproportionately impacted Iraqi civilians, who, it can be argued, were victims of Hussein's government and its decision to invade Kuwait as well. It is difficult to ascertain exactly what public opinion was about the invasion because of restrictions on free speech and fears on the part of Iraqis of retribution for speaking out, but there is evidence that it was not widely supported. Nonetheless, the Iraqi civilians paid a very heavy toll.

Another way that the war negatively impacted Iraq and Iraqis was through the imposition of economic sanctions. United Nations Resolution

661 imposed strict sanctions on Iraq immediately after the invasion, and even when the war ended and Iraq had withdrawn from Kuwait, these were not lifted. The sanctions excluded items related to humanitarianism, including food and medical supplies, but nonetheless, they caused widespread poverty that led to many deaths. The sanctions also made it more difficult for Iraq to rebuild in the aftermath of the war. The sanctions and their impact were especially dangerous in a country whose leadership had demonstrated little respect for large portions of its own population, particularly ethnic and religious minorities.

In addition to actions on the part of the UN and the United States that caused long-term issues, Iraq also did things during the war that were felt long after the peace agreements. One of the biggest was the setting of the Kuwaiti oil fields on fire. Because oil is so explosively flammable, and because there were land mines and other obstacles all around the oil fields, it was nearly impossible to put the fires out. Therefore, the fields burned and burned for months; they were not extinguished until November 1991 (by private firms). The losses in money were incredibly extensive, but more than that, the fires caused untold environmental damage. They also greatly impacted the air quality in the entire region for years to come.

There were also accusations of atrocities on both sides. In particular, Iraqis were accused of torturing coalition prisoners of war, which was strictly prohibited by the Geneva Convention. Several prisoners who were released at the end of the war described horrendous conditions and unimaginable crimes committed against them. A female flight surgeon also alleged that she was sexually assaulted while in Iraqi custody. These events loomed large in Americans' minds, especially when war with Iraq once again presented itself a little over a decade later.

Another controversial event during the war came to be known as the Bulldozer Assault. When American and other coalition forces entered Iraq, they faced labyrinths of land mines, barbed wire, and other obstacles, including trenches. These trenches housed many Iraqi troops. Rather than engaging in combat, a few of the units chose instead to bulldoze over the trenches, burying about 500 Iraqi men inside alive. The Americans suffered no casualties using the tactic, but there is evidence they thought what they were doing was wrong: they would not let reporters or other civilians witness the bulldozing.

Finally, another result of the Persian Gulf War that had a long-lasting impact was Operation Southern Watch. Under this program, the United States left approximately 5,000 of its own troops stationed in Saudi Arabia. This might not seem like a big deal (especially considering that there are more than 34,000 American troops stationed in Germany, a much smaller country), but it was an affront to many Muslims. Remember, Saudi Arabia is home to Medina and Mecca, the holy cities in Islam. The fact that there was a permanent military presence nearby was abhorrent to many. It was one of the causes that Osama bin Laden cited when he justified the attacks of September 11, 2001.

From a foreign relations standpoint, the Gulf War marked a turning point for the United States away from its direction during the Cold War. Instead of acting unilaterally, it appeared that the United States had allowed the United Nations to call the shots and acted accordingly. In contrast, during the Cold War, the U.S. often acted against UN wishes or stated policies and used covert and paramilitary operations to get what they wanted on the foreign stage. The U.S. also complied at the end of the war, allowing Hussein to remain in power and the government of Iraq to remain independent from much additional outside influence.

In reality, as we have seen, this narrative ignores some of the facts of the history of the war. For one thing, the United States was extremely powerful within the United Nations. Many countries relied on the U.S. for various kinds of aid and protection and instructed their representatives to vote along with the U.S. in the UN. The U.S. expected and demanded this kind of compliance from allies. In addition, the U.S. held several important seats on various UN committees that were involved in making decisions and issuing resolutions in the Persian Gulf War. At times, it is difficult to determine whether the United Nations led the United States, or the other way around. The United States also led the military operations and largely commanded the entire invasion.

All of that being said, the Gulf War did set a precedent for foreign relations moving forward. The United States was the indisputable global leader and acted in close concert with the United Nations. Many expected this type of action to continue, but the practice would be short-lived. After the terror attacks of September 11, 2001, the United States switched gears and again began acting unilaterally, ostensibly in pursuit of terrorism around the world.

Chapter Nine

Operation Iraqi Freedom

"How many additional American casualties is Saddam worth? . . . Not that many. So, I think we got it right, both when we decided to expel him from Kuwait, but also when the President made the decision that we'd achieved our objectives and we were not going to get bogged down in the problems of trying to take over and govern Iraq."

—Dick Cheney, 1992

Years after Operation Desert Storm, the Persian Gulf War was headline news again. In 2002-2003, George W. Bush, the son of George H. W. Bush, was himself president of the United States and seeking to do what his father had not: take out Saddam Hussein and establish a democratic government in Iraq. It is important to briefly cover these events since the two conflicts are so often discussed together.

George W. Bush's plan, called Operation Iraqi Freedom, sparked an uproar of controversy in the United States and around the world. In the aftermath of the Al Qaeda terror attacks on September 11, 2001, Americans and the world were extremely nervous about any unrest or brutality in the Middle East. Since Al Qaeda originated there and had ties to several powerful governments, many feared the region as a whole. What was more, Americans desired revenge against those who had killed so many of their own.

On the other hand, many Americans, as well as people and governments around the globe, objected to the plan for a variety of reasons. Chief among them were the chaos that would ensue for civilians in Iraq and beyond and the unconvincing evidence of Iraqi nuclear weapons or the means with which to produce them (which the invasion never yielded). When George W. Bush sought allies, he had much less luck than his father. His administration only managed to cobble together a meager alliance.

Many people well-remembered the controversial decision not to oust Saddam Hussein from power in 1991. Had that inaction put the world in danger, as the present Bush administration insisted? Despite objections, the invasion took place. After seven years of combat, more than 4,000 American deaths, tens of thousands of Iraqi civilians killed, and untold suffering and destruction, the next U.S. president, Barack Obama, ended the war. That said, as of 2021, there are still American troops stationed in Iraq, the region has not fully recovered, and the government is still dangerously unstable.

The timing of the Gulf War at the end of the Cold War was significant because it set a precedent for how the world would handle conflicts moving forward. With the end of the Cold War, America was the leader of the world, and Americans no longer feared a major rival. However, it would be short-lived. The rise of terror organizations such as Al Qaeda and the ways in which America responded to them guaranteed this. Unfortunately, conflict in the twenty-first century became closely associated with the Middle East. To this day, the entire region is often the site of violence and unrest.

Conclusion

In many ways, the Gulf War was the first major diplomatic challenge after the collapse of the Soviet Union. As such, it was a hugely important event in the history of twentieth-century foreign affairs. As we have seen, it set an important precedent, albeit one that would not last into the twenty-first century.

But the Gulf War was important on its own, even taken apart from the precedent that it set. Had Saddam Hussein been successful in maintaining control over Kuwait, much might be different today about the global supply of oil. In addition, there is no telling how far the war may have expanded had Hussein been appeased or allowed to continue unabated. He may have been successful in his invasion of Saudi Arabia, and a long, costly, and bloody conflict may have erupted in the Middle East, once again plunging the world into war.

It is impossible to know other outcomes. Nonetheless, the Persian Gulf War had long-lasting effects on the politics and foreign relations of the Middle East and the world. It continued to impact people for more than a decade after its end. It also changed the way the world responded to threats and acts of war, if only for a short time.

Bibliography

Atkinson, R. (1994). *Crusade: The Untold Story of the Persian Gulf War.*

Bacevich, A. J. (2016). *America's War for the Greater Middle East: A Military History.*

Blaydes, L. (2020). *State of Repression: Iraq Under Saddam Hussein.*

Coughlin, C. (2005). *Saddam: His Rise and Fall.*

Natsios, A. S., and A. H. Card, Jr. (2021). *Transforming Our World: President George H. W. Bush and American Foreign Policy.*

Onea, T. (2013). *US Foreign Policy in the Post-Cold War Era: Restraint versus Assertiveness from George H.W. Bush to Barack Obama.*

Polk, W. R. (2006). *Understanding Iraq: The Whole Sweep of Iraqi History, from Genghis Khan's Mongols to the Ottoman Turks to the British Mandate to the American Occupation.*

Razoux, P. and N. Elliott. (2015). *The Iran-Iraq War.*

Made in United States
North Haven, CT
13 December 2023

45482759R00036